Greenhouse Management

A FINE SPRING DISPLAY OF DAFFODILS, AZALEAS AND PRIMULAS

AMATEUR GARDENING PICTURE BOOK NO 10

GREENHOUSE MANAGEMENT

J. P. WOOD, N.D.H.

W. H. & L. COLLINGRIDGE LIMITED LONDON

FIRST PUBLISHED 1959

The Amateur Gardening Picture Books
are published by
W. H. & L. Collingridge Limited
2-10 Tavistock Street London W.C.2
and printed and bound in England by
Vandyck Printers Bristol and London
and James Burn & Co. Limited
London and Esher

OTHER AMATEUR GARDENING
PICTURE BOOKS

No. 1 Chrysanthemums

No. 2 Roses

No. 3 Tomatoes

No. 4 Plant Propagation

No. 5 Herbaceous Borders

No. 6 Garden Making (Double size)

No. 7 Dahlias

No. 8 Indoor Plants

No. 9 Pruning

Contents

Foreword   6

Greenhouse Types   8

Stagings   11

Greenhouse Heating   13

Ventilation   18

Damping Down   20

Shading   21

Seed and Potting Composts   22

Sterilizing Soil   24

Preparing Seed and Potting Composts   28

Seed Sowing   29

Pricking Out   34

Potting   36

Labelling   42

Soil Blocks   43

Stem Cuttings   43

Leaf Cuttings   48

Propagators   50

Watering   51

Forcing   53

Pest and Disease Control   54

Frames   58

John Innes Formulae and Notes   60

Foreword

by A. G. L. Hellyer F.L.S., Editor of *Amateur Gardening*

In the last few years there has been an enormous increase of interest in greenhouse plants. A great many gardeners have purchased greenhouses, perhaps in the first instance intending to use them simply for the raising of early seedlings and the cultivation of a summer crop of tomatoes. Before long they have discovered the great variety of fascinating exotic plants that can be cultivated with very little difficulty and no great expenditure on heating and their horizons have been correspondingly widened.

But though it is true that tender plants are not, as a rule, any more difficult to grow than those that are fully hardy, it is equally true that any plant in a pot requires more attention, and more skilled attention at that, than a similar plant growing in the open ground. It is much more sensitive to many things; to changes of temperature, atmosphere and moisture, to feeding and to the texture of the soil in which it is growing.

Hence the need for sound and simple instruction on the elements of greenhouse management. Many books have dealt with these matters but none, I fancy, is so likely to be helpful to the beginner as this largely pictorial account by Mr J. P. Wood.

To begin with Mr Wood has had considerable experience in the handling of greenhouse plants in several of the finest training establishments in the country; at Dartington Hall in Devon, at the John Innes Horticultural Institution in Hertfordshire, and in the Royal Horticultural Society's gardens at Wisley, Surrey. This practical experience in the handling of greenhouse plants has been followed by years of equally practical experience in advising amateur gardeners in their many problems. Since 1952 he has been one of my Assistant Editors on the staff of *Amateur Gardening* and his duties have been concerned very largely with the answering of readers' enquiries.

In the preparation of this book he has been able to make free use of the magnificent library of photographs which has been built up for *Amateur Gardening* over the years. I do not believe that any comparable collection exists elsewhere and it is gratifying to see these pictures finding a new use in this practical series of *Amateur Gardening* Pictorial Guides.

I recommend the book with confidence to anyone who has recently acquired a greenhouse or is thinking of doing so, and I believe that it will also be read with profit and pleasure by many old hands.

Acknowledgments

The author wishes to thank the following firms for the use of their photographs: The Metallic Constructions Co. (Derby) Ltd, James Blezard & Sons Ltd, Jones & Attwood Ltd, Agricultural Supplies (Cambridge) Ltd, Messrs P. J. Bryant, Chase Protected Cultivation Ltd.

Greenhouse Management

A greenhouse is a valuable asset in any garden and its uses are many. It not only extends the range of ornamental plants that can be grown but it also enables choice fruits and vegetables to be cultivated, such as grapes, peaches, melons, tomatoes and cucumbers.

It is a common fault for the beginner to attempt the cultivation of too many different subjects in a small greenhouse. Conditions that may suit one plant may not be satisfactory for another. Tomatoes, for instance, like warm, light conditions whereas cucumbers need a hot, moist and shady greenhouse. It is, therefore, undesirable to grow the two together in the same house. A scheme should be worked out at the outset and plants chosen that will thrive together in the conditions that can be provided.

The positioning of the greenhouse must also be given careful consideration. Although it is desirable to have it close to the house for convenience it must be placed in a position that receives all available natural light and not where it is likely to be in the shade of trees or other buildings. This is particularly important when the light intensity is low and the days are short in winter.

The greenhouse and cold frames in the picture below have been so placed that they receive plenty of light and are not in the shade of trees or buildings.

GREENHOUSE TYPES

There are various types of greenhouse from which to choose and the span roof house (above) is one of the most popular. The walls of the one shown are constructed with weather boarding at the base and the rest is glazed. This is an ideal greenhouse for growing plants in pots on a staging fixed level with the top of the wooden boarding.

Where there is a wall of sufficient height a lean-to greenhouse (left) can be built against the wall. A south facing wall is best and against it peaches and nectarines can be trained, with staging at the front of the house on which pot plants

can be grown. The $\frac{3}{4}$-span greenhouse, shown in the lower picture on the right is a modification of the two types already mentioned. It makes use of a wall and has all the advantages of a lean-to as well as admitting extra light from the $\frac{3}{4}$-span roof.

The greenhouse shown above is ideal for growing crop plants in beds such as tomatoes, lettuce or chrysanthemums. The large panes of glass admit the maximum amount of light into the greenhouse, although with this amount of glass heat is likely to be lost more quickly, compared with the other types, and heating this type of green-

9

house may well be more expensive.

The framework of a greenhouse is usually made of wood or metal alloy. Aluminium alloy houses have the advantage that painting is not necessary as it is with wooden structures which may need painting every two or three years. Also, as the glazing bars of metal greenhouses are comparatively slim, there is the minimum obstruction to light.

The greenhouse in the picture on the left has been divided into two parts with a glass partition and a door for access. This arrangement enables plants needing cool conditions to be grown in one part, and if more heating equipment is installed in the other section, plants that need more warmth can also be accommodated. As a temporary measure a greenhouse can be divided into two sections by means of plastic sheeting stretched across the greenhouse so that one part can be kept warmer or more moist than the other.

STAGINGS

These must be made stoutly as they have to carry a heavy load when covered with pots and boxes. Corrugated asbestos sheets covered with shingle or weathered ashes, as shown in the lower pictures on the previous page, are ideal for greenhouse staging and they can rest on concrete, wood or iron legs and supports.

The tiered staging on the right is particularly suitable for a lean-to or $\frac{3}{4}$-span greenhouse and plants can be kept close to the light. It also enables plants to be arranged decoratively.

The lower picture on this page shows the interior of a propagating house. Greenhouses of this type are sometimes called 'pits' as they are partly sunk below ground level. Apart from being used for

plant propagation a 'pit' is also ideal for the cultivation of melons and cucumbers which like a lot of moisture in the atmosphere. Underneath the staging, which is arranged on either side of a central path, it is usual to have hot-water pipes which provide 'bottom heat' for plants growing on the staging.

Beds of soil can be made on the staging in any type of house on which to grow crops such as lettuce, tomatoes, cucumbers or melons. In the top picture winter lettuce are being grown on the staging of a cold greenhouse. To give extra protection the raised beds are covered with cloches. These are normally used out of doors but in a greenhouse they also make a useful propagating frame.

Shelves slung from the greenhouse roof, as shown in the middle picture on the left, are always useful but particularly so in the spring when all available space is needed in the greenhouse. Boxes of seedlings can be stood closely on the shelves where the plants will receive plenty of light. It is also a good place to put plants, such as nerines, when they are resting.

Orchids, during their growing season, like a moist and airy atmosphere. To provide these conditions special staging can be made for the plants. It consists of a lower platform covered with moisture holding material, such as shingle or weathered ashes, and the plants are stood above it on slatted staging. This special type of staging is shown in the lower picture on the left. An alternative method is to stand the orchids on inverted pots placed on ordinary, ash-covered staging.

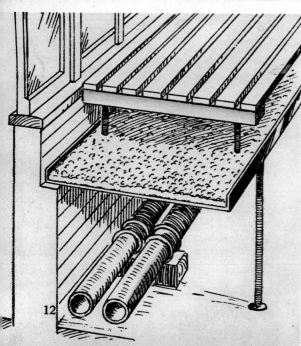

GREENHOUSE HEATING

To conserve heat in a greenhouse it is wise to insulate the side walls. This can be done by lining the inside with glasswool, as shown in the left hand picture above. The material can then be held in place with sheets of asbestos which is being done in the top right hand picture.

It is always advisable to have a thermometer in the greenhouse to check the temperature. A maximum and minimum thermometer is being 'set' in the picture on the right with a small magnet. This enables the indexes to be moved to the top level of the mercury in the two tubes. As the temperature rises the index in the right hand tube is pushed upwards but when the mercury falls the index remains behind to indicate the highest temperature. The same happens in the left hand or 'minimum' tube to indicate the lowest temperature.

13

The pictures on this page show three different kinds of heating apparatus using solid fuel. Above is a warm air stove showing the firebox and chimney on the outside of the greenhouse (right) and the rear of the stove, which is a hot air radiator, inside the greenhouse (left). The conventional way of heating a greenhouse is with a boiler and hot water pipes. The boiler must be outside the greenhouse, preferably covered in and well lagged, as shown in the lower left hand picture. The boiler in the lower right hand picture has a hopper for fuel and it will burn for 12-18 hours without attention.

Electricity provides the cleanest and most labour saving way of heating and there are many different types of heater. Tubular heaters, shown in the top right hand picture, are popular and they can be obtained in various lengths with a loading of 60 watts per foot. Their main disadvantage is that they have a fairly high surface temperature and plant foliage must be kept away from them. An electric convector heater is shown above on the left. It consists of an electric element enclosed in a cabinet. Air is drawn in at the base by a fan, is heated by the electric element and discharged at the top. The electric immersion heater is very useful for converting an existing hot water and boiler system to a more labour saving electrical system. The heating element of the model, shown in the lower picture, is fitted direct into the 4 in. hot water pipes. This model also has a thermostat built into the unit. The heater is supplied fitted to a U-bend and the unit is available in several different sizes.

15

Two other portable electric heaters are shown above. The one on the left is composed of an electric element and a fan which blows warm air out into the greenhouse and so ensures an even distribution of heat. The convector heater on the right can be fitted with a water tray if desired to prevent the atmosphere becoming too dry. This, however, is not likely to occur in the winter when the heater is used most in the average small greenhouse.

Apart from air or space heating the soil can be warmed by electric means to provide

'bottom heat'. The wires are connected to a transformer to reduce the voltage. The equipment is particularly useful for a propagating bench on which seed trays or pots of cuttings can be stood, as shown in the bottom picture on the previous page. The wires are laid on a bed of sand and covered with more sand. The whole is then covered with a layer of moist peat in which the pots or boxes can be sunk.

It is advisable to have a thermostat connected to the system so that it is automatic. The rod-type thermostat, shown above on the right, is more accurate although more expensive to purchase than the box type shown above on the left. The other thermostat in the centre (above) is for use with soil warming equipment.

Portable oil heaters are very useful for excluding frost from a cold greenhouse. An oil radiator is shown on the right. It is most important that all oil heaters are looked after well, otherwise

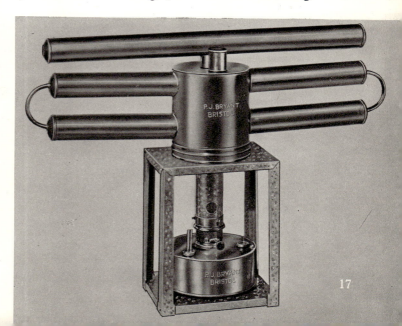

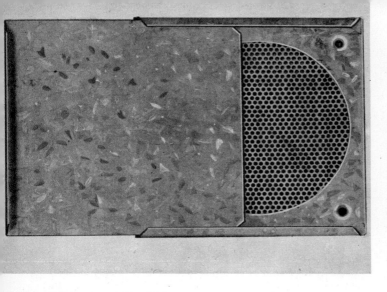

harmful fumes may be produced which may damage some plants severely.

In small, well built greenhouses the heater may not burn correctly at night because it is not getting a sufficient supply of air. This can be overcome by leaving a roof ventilator open slightly or a special ventilator, which can be seen on the left, can be fitted into the greenhouse wall.

VENTILATION

The principle of convection governs the system of ventilation in a greenhouse unless fans or similar extractor devices are introduced. When air is heated it expands and rises causing cooler air to be drawn in below. The drawing below shows, by means of arrows, how the air behaves in a well-ventilated greenhouse. Cold air entering the greenhouse by means of the lower ventilators is heated, either by the sun or the heating system, and as it expands it rises to escape through the ventilators in the roof. The three types of ventilator that can be fitted to a greenhouse can be seen in the top illustration on

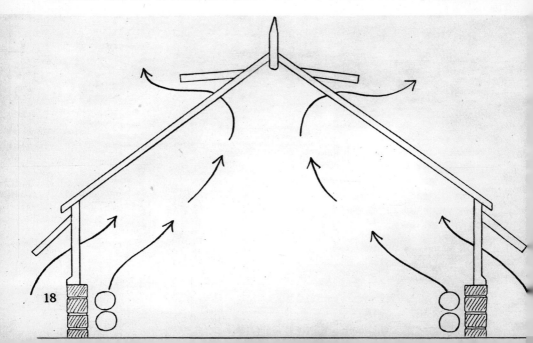

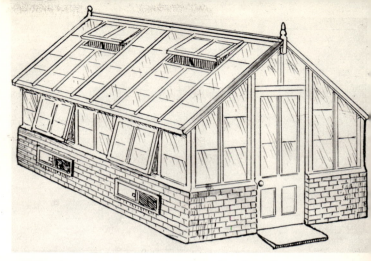

this page. The 'box' ventilators, fitted into the brick walls below the level of the staging, are very useful when the weather is cold and windy. In these conditions it is often difficult to use the other ventilators without causing cold draughts inside the greenhouse. As the air enters through the box ventilators it is warmed slightly on passing over the hot water pipes or electric heating tubes, where these are fitted, and so cold draughts are avoided. All greenhouses have ridge ventilators which are fitted into the roof on either side of the ridge board. There should be at least one on each side of the roof, depending on the size of the greenhouse. The side ventilators in the glass walls between the brickwork and the guttering are for use mainly in the summer when the weather is very hot.

The lower picture on this page shows a large lean-to greenhouse with only two small roof ventilators set too low on the slope. These are totally inadequate for maintaining good growing conditions. This greenhouse should have been made with one long continuous roof ventilator at the apex of the roof.

DAMPING DOWN

To maintain good growing conditions in a greenhouse the moisture in the atmosphere must be controlled. This is done simply by applying water to the floors, stagings and walls inside the greenhouse with a watering can as shown in the top picture on the left. It may be necessary to do this several times during a hot day in the summer and it not only helps to cool the greenhouse but it prevents the plants losing moisture too rapidly. In the lower picture on this page the staging and the spaces between the pots are being sprayed with water to maintain humid conditions. The temperature and the atmosphere in the greenhouse can, therefore, be controlled by ventilation and damping down. In the winter, however, when temperatures are low, very little damping is necessary and the aim should be to maintain drier conditions. Plants grow very slowly in the winter and a cold, damp and stuffy atmosphere is undesirable. To avoid this the greenhouse should be ventilated carefully.

SHADING

Another way of lowering the temperature in a greenhouse when the weather is hot is by means of shading. Also, many tender plants, such as orchids, cyclamen and primulas, would be scorched by strong sunshine unless they were shaded. The best way of shading a greenhouse is by means of roller blinds made with wooden laths as shown on the right. Hessian blinds are also good and they can be raised or lowered according to the brightness of the day.

Wooden lath blinds are useful in the winter as well when they can be lowered at night if the weather is cold to help keep the greenhouse warm.

Blinds are usually an expensive extra for a greenhouse and a cheaper method of shading is to apply a proprietary distemper, sold specially for the purpose, on the outside glasswork. This is done in the spring or early summer, as shown in the lower right hand picture. The shading should be washed off in early autumn as plants need all the available light in the winter.

For temporary shading tiffany or butter muslin can be fixed inside the greenhouse, as illustrated in the lower left hand picture.

21

SEED AND POTTING COMPOSTS

To be able to grow plants well in pots or boxes they need a suitable soil mixture or compost. If ordinary garden soil is used results are not likely to be very good and so it is important to prepare seed and potting composts carefully. Many gardeners have their own particular mixtures for different plants but thanks to the work of the John Innes Horticultural Institution we now have what are known as standardized composts. The John Innes Composts are suitable for the majority of plants grown in a greenhouse, with the exception of orchids. The J. I. Seed compost is for seed raising and the three potting composts are basically the same and vary only in the amount of fertilizers and chalk added. J.I.P.2 contains double quantities of fertilizer and chalk and J.I.P.3 has a treble dose of fertilizer and chalk compared with J.I.P.1 which contains the basic amount. The formulae of the John Innes composts are given on page 60.

J.I.P.1 compost is usually used for potting plants into 3 inch pots; J.I.P.2 is used mainly for plants potted into 5 or 6 inch pots and for pricking out seedlings and J.I.P.3 is for plants potted in 10 inch pots, which are often used for the final potting of the chrysanthemums.

Loam is the main ingredient of the composts and it is best prepared by stacking thick grass turves so that they are grass side down, as shown in the top picture on the opposite page. This is best done in early summer and the grass should have rotted sufficiently in about six months time for the material to be used.

The lower picture on the opposite page shows granulated peat being thoroughly wetted before use. Peat is an important ingredient in the composts as it serves as a soil conditioner and also as a supplier of humus. The other important ingredient is coarse sand similar to the type shown above on the right. The sand in the lower picture on this page is too fine for J.I. composts. The purpose of the sand is to assist drainage

23

STERILIZING SOIL

The main purpose of sterilizing soil for a seed or potting compost is to kill off harmful organisms, such as those which cause damping-off of seedlings. The soil can be treated with a chemical or preferably it can be heated to kill the pests and diseases that might be present. The soil obtained from the stacked turves (see page 22) should be riddled through a $\frac{3}{8}$ inch sieve (left).

Formalin is one of the best chemicals to use and it is diluted by using 1 part in 49 parts of water. This solution can then be watered on the sieved soil spread out on a hard surface as shown in the lower left hand picture. Afterwards the soil should be thrown into a heap and be covered with sacking, shown immediately below, for a day or so and then turned with a shovel periodically. This is done to help disperse the fumes of the chemical.

Heating the soil is the best way of killing harmful pests and diseases. The soil should be raised to 180-200° F. as quickly as possible and held at this temperature for 10 minutes.

A simple method is to place fairly dry soil in a bucket with the base perforated. This can then be stood in a domestic copper in a similar manner to that shown above on the left.

Small proprietary soil sterilizers can be purchased similar to the model shown on the right. The soil is placed in a bag holding $\frac{1}{4}$ bushel and it fits into a container as shown in the top picture on the right. The bag rests on a perforated tray below which is fast boiling water. The container is covered with a lid in which a thermometer indicates the temperature inside. The water can be boiled with a paraffin heater, as in the lower right hand picture.

25

Another low pressure steam sterilizer, working on the same principal as the previous model, is shown immediately above. This holds approximately one bushel of soil and for heating the water a fire is lit in the firebox at the base. As the water boils steam percolates through the soil mass and it takes 1-1½ hours to reach the necessary temperature.

Two electric soil sterilizers are shown on the left. The one above has the heating elements cast into aluminium plates. The electrical loading is 1½ Kw. and the bushel of soil that it holds takes approximately 1½ hours to sterilize. The soil to be sterilized is loaded from the top and emptied through the bottom. The sterilizer shown below on the left holds half a bushel of soil which may take 2-3 hours to heat to 180° F. It has a 300 watt electric heating element at the base.

The advantages gained by sterilizing the soil are lost if dirty pots and boxes are used as these can harbour harmful organisms. It is therefore important that all receptacles should be sterilized by standing them in boiling water or they can be stood in a solution of formalin. The lower left hand picture shows a method of handling pots when standing them in boiling water.

After sterilizing a quantity of soil it may be noticed that a fungus is spreading through the soil as in the top picture on the right. This, although it may seem alarming, is a harmless fungus.

After steam sterilizing soil it should be sufficiently moist and ready for mixing into a compost. A handful when squeezed in the hand should hold together as shown in the lower right hand picture.

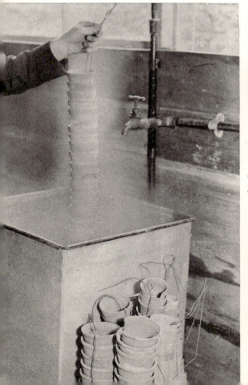

27

PREPARING SEED AND POTTING COMPOSTS

The different ingredients for the John Innes seed compost are shown above (the formula is given on page 60). To prepare the compost the loam is spread out evenly on a clean floor and then covered with the correct amount of peat and sand. A little of the sand is kept aside for mixing with the fertilizers so that they can be spread evenly over the heap. This is then turned with a clean shovel several times as shown below. It is most important that all the ingredients are thoroughly mixed together. The compost after mixing is ready for use and preferably it should not be stored for more than a month otherwise it may become too acid for some plants.

John Innes composts can be purchased ready mixed. Unfortunately, some makers do not always use the materials recommended and it is wise therefore to obtain the composts from a reliable source.

SEED SOWING

When sowing seeds in pots or boxes it is most important to provide good drainage. Failure to do this will result in a compost that is dank and stagnant and germination will be poor. Over the bottom of the pots clean crocks (broken pieces of pot) should be placed hollow side downwards, as shown in the picture on the right. The crocks can then be covered with a shallow layer of roughage—coarse peat or loam fibre is ideal. The seed compost can then be added to within approximately an inch of the top of the pot to leave space for watering later. As the compost is added firm it with the fingers and then level it off. To provide an even level surface for the seed a wooden presser can be used as in the lower picture on the right. The compost must not be firmed too hard otherwise the roots of the seedlings may not be able to penetrate in the compost satisfactorily.

29

A cross section of a prepared seed pan is shown in the top picture on this page and it shows clearly how to do the job correctly. Where a large amount of seed has to be sown, or when sowing fairly large seed which is to be spaced out, seed boxes 2 inches deep can be used. These should be prepared in exactly the same way as for a pot but the crocks should be laid along the crack at the bottom of the box. This can be seen in the middle picture on the left.

Before sowing the seed the compost must be well moistened and it is advisable to stand the containers in a shallow layer of water in a bath for a few moments. A seed box is being dipped in water in the lower left hand picture. Another method is simply to water the compost with a watering can fitted with a fine rose as in the top picture on the next page. It is advisable to allow the containers to stand for a little while before sowing the seed so that excess water can drain away. If the compost is thoroughly moistened in this way and quick germinating seeds such as annuals are being sown, it should not need watering again until after the seed has germinated.

The actual job of sowing the seed is not as simple as it may seem. The commonest fault is to sow too thickly which means the seedlings will be very over-crowded and they will become thin and spindly. In this condition they are very prone to 'damping-off' diseases. Try to sow the seed as thinly and evenly as possible over the whole surface of the compost. Starting from one end of the pot or box gently shake the seed from the packet on to the surface of the compost. Very fine seed, such as begonia and lobelia seed should not be covered with a layer of compost after sowing. Covering is usually necessary with larger seeds but in the case of carnations, which are sometimes raised from seed, a covering of silver sand can be given instead. Perpetual flowering carnation seed is being sown in the middle picture on this page and in the lower picture the seed is being covered with sand.

Seeds that are large enough to handle can be sown individually so that they are well spaced out. A convenient way of doing this is shown in the top left hand picture on the next page where dahlia seed is being sown from a sheet of glass. As the glass

is drawn along the box the seed is pushed off with the point of a knife or pencil on to the seed compost beneath. After sowing, the seed is covered with a shallow layer of finely sifted compost which is being done in the lower left hand picture.

To assist germination the seed containers are best stood in the warmest part of the greenhouse and each should be covered with a pane of glass as indicated in the lower picture on the right. It is also usual to put a covering of newspaper over the glass to prevent rapid drying out of the seed compost. Condensation will form on the underside of the glass and each day, until the seeds germinate, it should be removed to wipe away this condensation.

Sweet pea seeds are large enough to be handled individually but they are

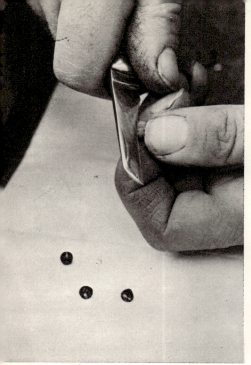

peculiar in that the seed coat is often very hard and this may hinder germination. This is common with varieties having black seeds and it is customary to 'chip' the seed covering with a knife as shown in the left hand picture above. Be careful not to injure the seed 'germ' when doing this.

To obtain early flowers and for exhibition purposes the seed is sown in October. Three inch pots can be used and each should be prepared as described on page 29. Four or five seeds can be sown in each pot and they should be buried approximately $\frac{1}{2}$ inch deep. A simple way is to make holes in the compost with a pencil, drop a seed into each hole, and cover with a little compost. Seeds are being sown in the top picture on the right and seedlings ready for potting can be seen in the picture on the right.

Different seeds take varying lengths of time to germinate but each day the glass and paper coverings should be removed, not only to wipe condensation from the glass, but also to see whether the seeds have germinated. When the seedlings appear the coverings must be removed otherwise they will grow thin and spindly. The top picture on the left shows the results of leaving the coverings on a seed box too long. Seedlings in this condition are useless and are best discarded.

Damping off is a soil borne disease that can damage young seedlings badly. It causes the delicate stems to shrivel at soil level and the seedlings topple over and die. Apart from sterilizing the loam for the seed compost Cheshunt compound can be watered on the compost before sowing. This preparation can be obtained from most garden shops and instructions for use are given on the containers.

PRICKING OUT

Seedlings should not remain too long in the seed pots or boxes for as they grow they need more space. Seven to 10 days after germination most seedlings should be transferred individually to another box. This is known as pricking out.

The boxes, which are usually a little deeper than the boxes used for seed sowing, should be prepared as already described on page 29 and 30 but John Innes Potting compost No. 2 should be used which contains more plant foods than the seed compost.

The level of the compost should be a little below the rim of the box and it can be made firm with a wooden presser as shown in the lower picture on the previous page.

The number of seedlings that are pricked out into the box will depend on the type of plant but the positions for each seedling can be marked if a special marking board is used as shown in the top picture on this page. It is not difficult to make a marker with a board to fit inside a standard size box; boot studs to make the impressions are nailed into the board.

The seedlings should be lifted carefully, one at a time, from the seed box and they should be held by the seed leaves and not by the stem. A hole is made with a dibber to take the seedling and then the compost is firmed around it, as shown in the picture on the right. Each seedling should be placed so that the seed leaves rest on the surface of the compost or a little above it.

35

POTTING

As plants grow they should be moved, step by step, into larger pots. It is a mistake to transfer a small plant direct into a large pot as it cannot utilize the large volume of soil all at once. This is why it is usual to pot plants from a 3 in. pot into 5 or 6 in. pots and later, where necessary, into 8, 9 or 10 in. pots. When a plant begins to fill its pot with roots it is time to pot it on into a larger pot.

Before potting, a few pieces of broken pot (crocks) should be placed over the drainage hole at the bottom of the pot as shown in the top picture on the right. Instead perforated zinc discs can be used as shown above on the left. In the lower left hand picture the crocks are being covered with a little rough peat or loam fibre to contain the potting compost. After adding a little compost the plant should be placed centrally in the pot and the fresh compost firmed around it with the fingers, as in the lower right hand

picture on the previous page, or with a wooden label as in the picture above on the left. The level of the compost must be a little below the rim of the pot to allow for watering.

The picture above on the right shows a chrysanthemum which has filled its 5 in. pot with roots. It is ready for its final move into a 10 in. pot. The existing crocks must be removed, as shown below on the left, and in the next picture the new compost is being made firm with a wooden rammer to secure tighter potting than would be possible with the fingers.

Before potting a plant from one pot into a larger one it is important that the compost is moist, otherwise it will not establish itself quickly in its new pot. Plants that are to be potted should be watered a little while before potting and afterwards they should not need watering again for a day or so.

Part of the skill in potting plants is to ensure that the compost is firmed evenly around the plant. If, because the compost is not firmed sufficiently, gaps or hollows are left in the compost, the plant will not be happy. In the picture above the plant on the left has made a good, even root system but because of bad potting the root system of the plant on the right is poor.

Begonias and gloxinias can be raised from seed but it needs to be sown in January or February in a greenhouse with a temperature of 60° F. to have good flowering plants in the same year. Alternatively tubers of these plants can be purchased when dormant. It is best to start them into growth by pressing them into a mixture of moist peat and coarse sand in a shallow tray. This is shown in the picture on the left. Begonia tubers have a depression on one side and this is the top side of the tuber.

Growth will soon begin if the tubers are kept in a warm, moist part of the greenhouse. The gloxinias in the picture above have made good growth and they are ready for potting separately in 5 in. pots as shown in the lower picture. Later the plants can be potted into 6 or 7 in. pots and the compost should be firmed gently with the fingers and not pressed too hard. During the summer the plants must be shaded from strong sunshine and the atmosphere kept moist by regular damping down. After flowering water should be withheld gradually until the compost is dry. The tubers are rested during the winter and started into growth again the following spring. When dormant they must be kept in a dry, frost proof place; dampness may cause the tubers to rot.

Hyacinths, daffodils and tulips are popular bulbs for giving a bright display in a greenhouse in the spring. Potting can be done in late August or early September and 5 or 6 in. pots are suitable. John Innes Potting compost can be used and crocks should be placed at the bottom of the pots to ensure good drainage. Afterwards partly fill with compost and press the bulbs into place. In the top picture on the left five daffodil bulbs have been placed in one pot and in the lower left hand picture three tulip bulbs are ready to be covered with compost. The bulbs must not be covered completely and the tips should be left above the final level of the compost.

Bulbs can also be grown in undrained bowls containing bulb fibre which contains peat, oyster shell and charcoal to prevent it becoming sour. This fibre must be thoroughly moistened before use. In the picture immediately below daffodils are

being pressed into moist fibre in a bowl.

Lilies also can be grown in pots for flowering in a cool greenhouse. The bulbs of stem rooting kinds, such as *L. auratum* and *L. speciosum* should be placed sufficiently low in the pot, shown in the top picture on the right, to allow for top dressing later as the stem develops.

Once the bulbs have been potted they must be given cool conditions for at least eight weeks to allow them to make good roots. It is best to plunge the pots outside under a layer of weathered ashes or peat as shown in the lower right hand picture. Once good roots have been made the pots can be moved to a cold frame and a little later transferred to a cool greenhouse. The bowls of bulbs in the lower left hand picture have recently been taken into the greenhouse where they are beginning to make strong new growth. A temperature of 45-50°F. is adequate at this stage.

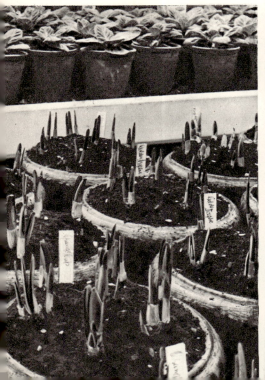

41

LABELLING

It is always wise to label plants clearly, particularly where cuttings of different varieties of a plant are being taken and where several different kinds of seed are being sown. It is surprising how easily plants can be muddled if they are not labelled. Seed boxes and pots should also carry a label and it is helpful if the date of sowing as well as the name of the plant is indicated. Labels can be purchased ready for use but if plain wood labels are used they should be given a coating of white lead paint. This can be done simply by rubbing the paint on the label with a piece of rag as shown in the above picture. If the labels are then written immediately the writing will set into the paint and last a long time. Use a black lead pencil for writing and not an indelible one otherwise the writing will soon smear if it becomes wet. There is a right and wrong way to write a label as illustrated on the left. If the name is printed from the top downwards it may be partly obscured when the label is in place.

LILIAN BARNES

LILIAN BAR

RIGHT

WRONG

SOIL BLOCKS

The use of soil blocks instead of pots has in recent years become popular and they have the advantage that planting out can be done with practically no root disturbance. Soil blocks do, however, need to be watered carefully as the outside of the block tends to dry out rapidly in hot weather. John Innes compost can be used to make the blocks and on this page three of the many machines for making the blocks are shown. The type above on the left makes a hexagonal block. To fill the mould it is thrust into the heap of compost and, after pushing down the lower lever to make the hole in the block for the plant, the top lever is pressed down to eject the soil block. An entirely different type of machine is shown on the right. It can be used to make a normal round soil block or the block can be made around a young plant. The machine on the right below is an inexpensive model and ideal for the amateur gardener requiring only a few blocks. As blocks are made they should be placed close to one another in a seed tray or box. If they are stood direct on the staging they are liable to crumble. When it is time to plant out, the trays containing the blocks can be transported with the minimum amount of disturbance.

STEM CUTTINGS

Although many greenhouse plants, such as cyclamen, primulas and cinerarias, are raised from seed, others are best propagated from cuttings. If, for example, seed was saved from a named fuchsia variety

43

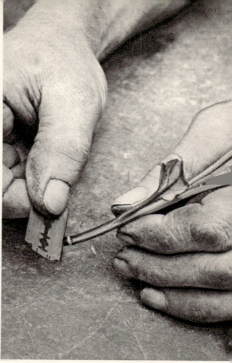

the seedlings are not likely to be identical with the parent, but if cuttings are taken the new plants will be the same as the plant from which the cuttings were secured.

Sturdy and firm unflowered shoots make the best cuttings and they should not be long and spindly. In the picture above on the left chrysanthemum shoots are being removed from the parent plant. The cuttings should be made about 3-4 in. long, and after removal of a few of the lower leaves, cut across the base of the shoot, immediately below a leaf joint, with a sharp knife or razor blade as shown in the above picture on the right. Prepared dahlia cuttings, taken from tubers started into growth in the greenhouse, are shown on the left.

Shown in the top left hand picture on the opposite page is a prepared coleus cutting, ready to be inserted in the

rooting mixture.

To assist cuttings to make roots they can be treated with a hormone rooting preparation. In the above picture on the right prepared cuttings are being dipped in a rooting powder—only the ends are treated.

To root cuttings successfully they must be inserted in a suitable compost or rooting medium. Pure sand is often used and the white Cornish grit, obtained from the washings of the China clay industry in Cornwall, is particularly good. Sand, however, contains no plant foods and so, once cuttings have rooted, they must be potted separately in a suitable potting compost, otherwise they will starve. This also applies to vermiculite which is an excellent rooting medium. A cutting compost which gives very good results is made up with 3 parts sand, 2 parts peat and 1 part loam.

45

The lower picture on the previous page shows sand being sprinkled over the surface of the cutting compost in a 3 in. pot and on the left it is being gently firmed with another small pot. The extra sand is to encourage rooting, as it trickles to the bottom of the dibber holes when the cuttings are inserted. This is being done in the lower left hand picture. It will be noticed that the cuttings are being inserted around the edge of the pot. The reason for this is to keep the lower part of the cutting close to the air which percolates through the porous clay pot. Air, moisture and warmth all help in the formation of roots. Many plants, such as chrysanthemums, will, however, root happily if the cuttings are inserted in boxes as shown immediately below.

Once cuttings are removed from the

parent plant they will soon wilt as, having no roots, they lose moisture more quickly than they can obtain it. To prevent serious wilting, the cuttings should be kept in a moisture ladened atmosphere in a propagating case or box until new roots have been made. This will help to keep the leaves turgid. The cuttings in the picture above are being given a good watering and the pots are partly sunk into moist peat inside the propagating case. Afterwards the frame light will be shut and newspaper spread over the glass to maintain equable conditions inside. Cuttings of different plants vary in the length of time that they take to make roots; when new white roots can be seen around the edge of the compost, as shown in the lower picture, it is time to pot them separately into 3 in.

LEAF CUTTINGS

Apart from increasing plants by means of cuttings there are several greenhouse subjects that can be propagated from their leaves. Chief among these are *Begonia rex*, saintpaulias, streptocarpus and gloxinias. The last are readily raised from seed but if a particularly fine form appears, and it is desired to increase the stock, leaf cuttings can be taken. A leaf with a piece of leaf stalk is being removed from a gloxinia in the top left hand picture. It is then inserted upright in sandy cutting compost in a pot or pan as shown above on the right. To encourage rooting the cuttings should be placed in a warm and humid propagating box or case. (These are described and illustrated on pages 49 and 50).

Saintpaulia leaf cuttings can be taken in a similar manner. Roots appear within a matter of weeks at the base of the

leaf stalk and from this point the new plant develops. Rooted saintpaulia leaves are shown in the lower picture on the previous page

The leaves of *Begonia rex* are treated differently. A mature leaf is removed from a plant and the veins on the under side are cut at intervals with a sharp knife. The prepared leaf is placed on the surface of a cutting compost in a seed box so that the cut veins are resting on the soil. To keep the cut parts in contact with the compost small stones or pieces of pot can be placed on the leaf. After watering, as shown in the picture above, the leaf cuttings are stood in a propagating box. Rooting takes place from the cut veins and several new plants can be obtained from a single leaf. Once good roots have been made each plant should be potted separately.

PROPAGATORS

To be able to increase plants successfully a propagating frame or box is indispensable in the greenhouse. It need not be an elaborate affair and it is perfectly feasible to make one at home from a wooden box. In the lower picture on the previous page cuttings have been inserted in a home-made propagator and the top is being covered with a sheet of glass to retain warmth and moisture. Another simple propagator is shown in the lower left hand picture on this page.

It is constructed over the hot water pipes in a greenhouse to provide bottom heat. A hinged glass lid has also been fitted. The bottom of a propagator is best covered with a layer of moist peat on which seed boxes can be stood or into which pots can be plunged. Alternatively the bottom can be filled with the cutting compost and cuttings can be inserted direct into the mixture. A more elaborate propagating frame is shown below on the right. It is heated electrically and a predetermined temperature can be maintained by means of a thermostat. A simple electric propagator is shown in the top illustration. It is primarily intended for germinating small amounts of seed. The seed compost is kept moist by means of the wick suspended in a dish of water.

WATERING

To be able to grow plants in pots well they must be watered carefully. They need sufficient moisture to prevent them from flagging or wilting but the compost must not be kept overwet for long periods. Each plant should be treated individually and it is a mistake to water all the plants in a greenhouse at once irrespective of whether they need water or not. For watering plants on a greenhouse staging a

can with a long spout holding a gallon of water is useful. A watering can of this type is shown above on the right. The water should not be poured into the pot forcibly, otherwise the compost will be washed out, and it is wise to use a rose on the can as shown in the lower left hand picture. There are several ways of telling whether a plant needs water. If the pot is tapped and the compost is dry a ringing sound will result. A dull muffled sound occurs if the compost is moist. A tapper can be made simply with a knob of wood, or a cotton reel on the end of a stick. A home made tapper is seen

51

in use in the lower right hand picture on the previous page. This method is not infallible as a cracked pot will tend to give a dull sound whether the compost inside is wet or dry. The appearance and feel of the compost will also indicate whether water is needed or not. If the compost appears dry the plant should be watered. Do not give a plant driblets of water, or in other words, a little and often, but fill to the top of the pot with water when it is needed. Give no more water until the compost again begins to dry out.

During the summer, when plants are growing rapidly and temperatures are higher, plants will need more water than in the winter. If it is doubtful whether a plant needs water in the summer it is wise to give water but in the winter it is better to defer watering until the following day.

Before potting a plant it should be given a good watering beforehand, then no more water should be needed for a few days. But when young seedlings are potted separately into small pots they do need watering immediately afterwards as they have only small root systems. A young seedling is being watered in the top picture on this page. A finger is held over the spout of the watering can to prevent the compost being disturbed unduly.

A simple method of automatic watering is by means of trickle irrigation equipment. This consists of tubing connected to a water supply and along the tubing small nozzles are fixed at intervals. Water gradually seeps through the nozzles to keep the soil around each plant

moist. This equipment is seen in use with pot plants in the lower picture on the previous page.

FORCING

The space beneath the greenhouse staging is very often wasted but it can be put to good use for forcing seakale and rhubarb.

In the top picture on this page seakale roots or crowns are being placed in boxes of old potting compost under greenhouse staging. The crowns are obtained from plants grown outside during the summer and in the autumn the plants are lifted and side roots are trimmed from the main roots. These are used for forcing. Instead of using boxes the seakale crowns can be placed in a 9 in. pot—six crowns can be forced in a pot of this size. The usual time to start forcing is in January. Seakale must be forced in complete darkness and light can be excluded by a curtain of sacking hung from the staging as in the lower picture. If seakale is grown in pots, light can be excluded by standing an inverted pot on the lower one, but the drainage hole must be plugged. Seakale can be forced early in a greenhouse with a minimum temperature of 45°.

The space under greenhouse staging can also be used for storing plants when they are dormant. Dahlia tubers are being packed under staging in the top picture on the next page. Plants in pots, such as gloxinias or tuberous begonias can also be laid on their sides under the staging for the winter, but in all these cases care must be taken to see that no water drips on them.

PEST AND DISEASE CONTROL

One of the most effective ways of dealing with pests and diseases is by fumigation. In the lower left hand picture nicotine concentrate is being poured into a metal saucer. This is heated by a small methylated spirits burner, as shown below on the right, and nicotine vapour soon fills the house. Nicotine will kill any greenfly present but as soon as the lamp is lit, leave the greenhouse and seal the door with sacking to prevent the fumes escaping, as shown in the lower left hand picture on the next page. All ventilators should be closed tightly before fumigation. Concentrated nicotine is very poisonous and it must be handled with due care.

Another way of fumigating a greenhouse is to use nicotine shreds. The shreds are laid on a stone and, after ignition, as shown in the top picture on the next page, are allowed to smoulder to produce

nicotine vapour.

Smoke bombs containing insecticides such as DDT and BHC and fungicides such as karathane and TCNB are very useful for dealing with insect pests and fungus diseases in the greenhouse. You must ascertain the cubic capacity of the greenhouse (indicated on page 60) and use only the appropriate size smoke bomb for it. The smoke bomb or cone is ignited by a fuse and a dense smoke is produced containing the insecticide or fungicide. This is shown in the lower right hand picture on this page. Full instructions are given with the smoke bombs indicating how they should be used and the precautions that should be taken. The best time of day for fumigation is in the evening and when the weather is calm. The greenhouse should not be opened again until the following morning when the ventilators can be opened wide.

The equipment shown above will probably have been seen in shops and restaurants. It is composed of an electrical heating element which surrounds a cup containing the insecticide. This is gradually discharged into the atmosphere and it helps considerably in keeping a greenhouse free of insect pests. The equipment is for hire only and cannot be bought outright.

Each year at the end of the growing season it is wise to clear out the greenhouse and scrub the structure with water containing disinfectant, as shown in the lower left hand picture. After scrubbing wash the dirt away by spraying with clear water. This is being done in the lower right hand picture.

After a time green slime and dirt tend to collect in the overlaps of the panes of glass and this reduces the light reaching plants within. To remove this slime use a thin piece of metal, such as a plant label, and work it up and down as shown in the picture above. To complete the cleansing the inside brickwork of the greenhouse can be limewashed. This is being done in the lower left hand picture. Dirt, and soot, particularly in industrial districts, accumulate quickly on the outside of a greenhouse and obscure light. Plants need all available light in the winter when the natural light intensity is low and it pays to wash the outside glasswork to remove the grime. A special mop is being used in the lower right hand picture.

FRAMES

A garden frame is a great asset used in conjunction with a greenhouse. Plants raised in the greenhouse can be hardened off (acclimatized to outside conditions) before they are planted in the open and it is also a useful place for keeping plants when not in flower or when they are resting. If one cannot afford a greenhouse, a frame, in fact, is the next best thing. The frame in the top picture on this page has wooden sides, sloping from front to rear, but the frame lights, although of robust construction, are heavy to handle. The frame is being ventilated by placing a block of wood under the light. A span roof frame is shown in the picture on the left. It is really a

miniature greenhouse and it is ideal for growing alpines in pots or pans, apart from a wide variety of greenhouse subjects.

Another span roof frame is shown above. This one is made of metal and as the glazing bars are narrow the frame is well lit inside. Here cucumbers are being grown as a summer crop and in the winter lettuce could be grown very well.

The frame shown on the right has the advantage of being portable. The wooden sides are covered with Dutch lights. These are composed of a wooden frame and a single pane of glass. Dutch lights have the advantage of being easy to move and as there are no glazing bars they admit plenty of light.

59

A selection of flower pots in general use showing the cast numbers and internal measurements in inches.

JOHN INNES SEED COMPOST

2 parts loam
1 part peat   } Parts by bulk
1 part sand

To each bushel of the mixture add 1½ oz. superphosphate of lime and ¾ oz. chalk.

JOHN INNES POTTING COMPOST

7 parts loam
3 parts peat   } Parts by bulk
2 parts sand

To each bushel of the mixture add ¼ lb. J.I. base fertilizer and ¾ oz. chalk.

To make J.I.P.2 and J.I.P.3 compost add double and treble amounts of fertilizer and chalk respectively to the basic formula (J.I.P.1), which is given above.

JOHN INNES BASE FERTILIZER

2 parts hoof and horn
2 parts superphosphate of lime   } Parts by weight
1 part sulphate of potash

JOHN INNES LIQUID FEED

15.00 parts ammonium sulphate
2.75 parts potassium nitrate   } Parts by weight
2.25 parts mono-ammonium phosphate

Use ½—1 oz. of the feed per gallon of soft water

Notes

The internal measurements of a bushel box are 22 in. × 10 in. × 10 in.

To ascertain the cubic capacity of an equal span greenhouse multiply the length by the breadth by the average height. To obtain the latter, measure the height to the ridge board and add to the height of one side wall. Divide the result by two.